Seasons of a Lifetime

Seasons of a Lifetime

A Treasury of Meditations

Gerhard E. Frost

Augsburg • *Minneapolis*

SEASONS OF A LIFETIME
A Treasury of Meditations

Scripture quotations unless otherwise noted are from the Revised Standard Version of the Bible, copyright 1946, 1952, and 1971 by the Division of Christian Education of the National Council of Churches.

Poems from Logos Art Productions, copyright © 1986 Logos Art Productions Inc., Inver Grove Heights, MN 55076, are reprinted by permission.

Cover design: Lecy Design
Internal design: Patricia M. Boman

Library of Congress Cataloging-in-Publication Data

Frost, Gerhard E.
    Seasons of a lifetime : a treasury of meditations / Gerhard Frost.
        p.   cm.
    "Commemorative anthology"—Foreword.
    ISBN 0-8066-2452-3
    1. Meditations.   I. Title.
    BV4832.2F76   1989
    242—dc20
                                                                89-36045
                                                                CIP

The paper used in this publication meets the minimum requirements of American National Standard for Information Sciences—Permanence of Paper for Printed Library Materials, ANSI Z329.48-1984.   ∞™

Manufactured in the U.S.A.   AF 9-2452
93   4   5   6   7   8   9   10

Contents

Acknowledgments 7
Foreword 9

Spring Travelers 13
To Be Alive 14
I Believe 16
Meeting 16
I Need Her 17
Memento 18
Doxology 19
An Early Cry 20
All Flights Cancelled 22
Science Lecture 24
God's Kindergarten 25
Let's Play Baptism 26
The Difference 27
Heaven 28
We Have 29
Friends 30
Boxed In 31
Innocence 32
The Threat 33
The Demon Self-Doubt 34

One Race 36
Treasure the Child 37
Small Talk 38
Christmas Lesson 39
The Best Talk 40
Be Kind 41
Child Wisdom 42
Thresholds 43
Wow! 44
Cherries 44
Swaying Room 45
Just Think 46
Love Cheats 47
Jubilee 48
Do You Remember? 49
This Land of Leaving 50
We Won 51
Family Talk 52
Where Thought Breaks
    Down 53
Make Room 54

Summer Loose-Leaf 57
One Generation to
    Another 58
Making Love 59
Our Mystery 60
Love Talk 60
God's Way for Me 61
To Be a Friend 62
The Challenge 63
My Personal Devil 64
Lord, Help Me 65
The Lived Life 66
Home 68
A Dirty Word 69
Soggy Cereal and
    Tepid Tea 70
The Goal 72
One More 72
Homecoming 73

I Am Found 74
We Live on Glimpses 75
Frightened 76
Made in God's Image 76
How Comforting 77
Alive Again 78
Only Sometimes 79
Only Visiting 80
Earth's Cry 82
The Movement of
    Grace 83
Idolatry 84
Forgiveness 84
A Lesson 85
Our Lord Says, "Go!" 86
The Way We Turn 87
Why 87
Let Us Give Thanks 88
Disguise 90

Autumn   I'm Glad 93
I Understand 94
Everything Is Different 95
Rejoice with Me 96
Sunrise 98
Maturity 99
To the Perpetual Critic 100
Dead 100
I've Begun Asking 101
Prayer 102
Knowledge 103
Zero 104
Can This Be? 105
I Met a Man 106
"I've Missed You" 108
What Shall I Say? 109
I Wasn't Ready 110

Her Gift 111
Look Again 112
Trusting 113
Our Distant Drummer 114
I'm the One 114
God's Shut-In 115
Seven Seconds 116
Diminished 117
Thank You, Lord 118
A Simple Man 119
Love Knows 119
Going On 120
Grounds for Hope 121
Worship 122
Whose Dream Am I? 123
I Wasn't Afraid 124
Joker 126
Never Too Busy 128

Winter   I Hear a Voice 131
Lonely 132
Anniversaries 133
Reverie 134
He Hanged Himself 134
Retired 135
Autobiography 135
The Seed 136
Small Change 138
Two Journeys 139
All Must Fall 140
My Country 141
Servant 141
Help Us to Let Go 142
Toughest Fact 143
God's Perennials 143
What I Don't Like About
    Jesus 144

The Music of the Mind 145
The Reason 145
For His Age 146
Lord, I Saw Two 147
Saturday Morning 148
Riches 149
The Hardest Part 150
Memory 151
And a Half 152
God Knows 153
Lost 154
As I Bow 154
Nebo 155
Celebration 156
Years Are Kettles 157
Two Words 158
Three with a Secret 159
Home Sounds 160

Acknowledgments

In addition to new, previously unpublished meditations, this volume collects many Gerhard Frost meditations that were originally published in these books:

From *Blessed Is the Ordinary* (Minneapolis: Winston Press, 1980): To Be Alive, All Flights Cancelled, Science Lecture, Christmas Lesson, Be Kind, Love Cheats, We Won, Where Thought Breaks Down, One Generation to Another, God's Way for Me, Frightened, Alive Again, Let Us Give Thanks, I Understand, Going On, I Wasn't Afraid, The Seed, Saturday Morning.

From *A Second Look* (Minneapolis: Winston Press, 1985): I Need Her, God's Kindergarten, Treasure the Child, Swaying Room, Just Think, Making Love, My Personal Devil, Home, Only Visiting, Everything Is Different, I've Begun Asking, I Met a Man, "I've Missed You," I'm the One, Grounds for Hope, Whose Dream Am I?, Joker, Autobiography, Help Us to Let Go, The Music of the Mind, Years Are Kettles, Two Words.

From *Bless My Growing* (Minneapolis: Augsburg Publishing House, 1974): An Early Cry, The Demon Self-Doubt, The Lived Life, Soggy Cereal and Tepid Tea, One More, We Live on Glimpses, The Movement of Grace.

From *Kept Moments* (Minneapolis: Winston Press, 1982): The Difference, We Have, Boxed In, The Threat, Small Talk, Child Wisdom, Family Talk, The Challenge, The Goal, A Lesson, Disguise, Prayer, Look Again, Diminished, Never Too Busy, Reverie, All Must Fall, Lost.

From *Homing in the Presence* (Minneapolis: Winston Press, 1978): Thank You, Lord; Lord, I Saw Two.

From *What in the World Are We Doing?* (Minneapolis: Logos Art Productions, 1987): One Race.

From *It Had Better Be True* (Minneapolis: Logos Art Productions, 1986): Lonely, God Knows.

From *Hungers of the Heart* (Minneapolis: Logos Art Productions, 1986): Thresholds; Make Room; Lord, Help Me; As I Bow.

From *Deep in December* (Minneapolis: Logos Art Productions, 1986): Small Change, The Hardest Part.

From *God's Way for Me* (Minneapolis: Logos Art Productions, 1986): This Land of Leaving, The Way We Turn, Maturity, Anniversaries, Toughest Fact.

From *You Are Blessed* (Minneapolis: Logos Art Productions, 1986): To Be a Friend.

From *Silent Spaces* (Minneapolis: Logos Art Productions, 1986): Only Sometimes, What Shall I Say?

Foreword

*Gerhard Emanuel Frost, my father, died of cancer
May 23, 1987, at the age of 78. Until two weeks
before his death, he kept up his writing and public
speaking, and in the final days he made his good-
byes to many friends, colleagues, and family
members. His last words to two in his family were,
"Forgive everything. Remember the best."*

"Remembering the best" is what this book, Seasons
of a Lifetime, *is all about. While most of Dad's
published work was written in his later years, it
notes some of his own best memories of a lifetime,
as well as some painful ones. And he writes about
moments in the lifetimes of people whose lives
touched his.*

*This commemorative anthology includes most of the
favorite poems of members of Gerhard's immediate
family, as we "remember the best." It also includes
more than 50 unpublished poems we recently
discovered.*

*We had our pick of favorites, but often we didn't
agree with each other. Then we took a vote. We are
sorry we couldn't include Gerhard's readers in our
informal poll. If you are already familiar with his
work, we hope you'll find in this volume at least
some of the poems you too have liked best.*

These poems reflect many facets of a lifetime's seasons. And they catch some of the writer's persona: pastor, teacher, learner, lover of nature, child, parent, spouse, grandparent, friend.

And what about "forgive everything"? No one, of course, lives in this world without garnering reasons to be forgiven (and to forgive). But if you were to ask about this writer the question often asked about others—did he live the way he wrote?— we, his family, would say an emphatic "yes!" His spirit—which I believe endures—is the gentlest I've ever known, a gentleness supported by a firm belief in the God-given worth of every individual. This is my clearest image of my father as I "remember the best."

—Naomi Frost

Spring

Travelers

Two:
  Hi, world, I'm two;
  How old are you? Are you new too?
  Want to play, world, just me and you?
  You hide, I'll seek;
  I'll taste and smell, look and touch,
  and listen. I want the feel of you.
  I like you, world—you like me too?
  It's fun being two and friends with you!

Eighty-Two:
  Good-bye, world, I'm eighty-two;
  it's been nice, knowing you.
  But I'm leaving; I'm old, you see,
  and yet God makes me new as well as you.
  I'm sorry I hurt you, world,
  but you hurt me too.
  Let's play, like we used to do,
  a quiet game, just right for eighty-two:
  I forgive, and so do you.

To Be Alive

Only two,
a stranger to my "take-for-granteds,"
her days full of firsts,
and this was one:
my typewriter.

Seated on my lap
she stretched to reach the keys.
Her small finger found the hyphen,
striking it again and again
all across the page.

I held her high
so she could see.

"Mmm! Ants!" she said,
and looked 'round at me
in shared delight.
I looked, and there they were,
ants, little black ones,
marching single file
in their unwearying way.
There they were, also for me,
made free to image with her
in her world of glad discovery.

A few more seconds
of clicking and admiring
and she was on her way,
filled with the satisfaction
of success.

Measured by my standard,
touch-key grown-upness,
I would call it failure,
but what is it to succeed?
Isn't it to be alive,
to see more than there is,
to hear more than is said,
to be more than we are?

I Believe

I've been told, and I believe
that God has placed an ozone screen
without which nature's sun would only burn,
would scorch and sear,
instead of save.

Has this same God placed a baby's face
to guard us from the blinding, searing light
of holiness—the infant face of humankind,
the Bethlehem face? I've been told,
and I believe.

Meeting

A child's shrill voice, calling to
another across the street: "I'm not allowed
to cross the street, but I can meet you
in the middle!"

The trouble with rules is that they're
often smaller than people. They break themselves
upon the human situation.
Legalism at its worst forgets
that life is not confined nor confinable.
Where the spirit is greater than the rule,
we find a way to reach past it
in meeting.

I Need Her

I stood outside her door,
eavesdropped as she continued
the prayers we'd just been praying.
"God besh the whole forld!"
I heard her say.

I peeked—and in her hands
she held it all, the world—
her doll, her stuffed toy rabbit
and her teddy bear.

The smaller we are, the less we fear
the sweeping statement, the expansive promise
and exuberant response.

Today I'm captive to my cautious prayers,
my shackled mind, my grown-up heart.
I need her for my freedom, to rescue me
for high and holy places.

I need her too for courage
to receive this vast and frightening world
and look into a dark abyss
more frightening still—
my untrusting heart.

Memento

My friend travels a lot,
this time to Chicago.
He'd packed with care,
but when he opened his case
in the hotel
he found two small, white shoes.
Scruffy and bedraggled, they were
placed there by dimpled hands
of one who wanted to be with Daddy.

Two little shoes—a memento of home;
they lent purpose and pertinence
to grown-up business.

Doxology

Thank you, God Almighty,
for the glory,
the love-filled emptiness
at the beginning;
for the ordered fullness,
the warming pulse-beat
and the budding brainpower
in the continuing.

Thank you for the once-for-all
conception, birth and life,
the death and resurrection,
the victorious ascension
and reigning presence of the Son.

And thank you for the witness
of the Spirit in our hearts
when we cry: "Abba—Daddy—Father!"

An Early Cry

Two years old and, true to us all,
she loved a story.
Her name: Rachel, but when she said it,
it came out as "Rechu."

On this particular evening
nothing was right;
bumps, bruises, frustrations and disappointments
had drawn her to me,
and she stood with her curly head
bent into my lap,
hiding two tear-stained cheeks.

It was then that I said,
"Shall Granddaddy tell you a story
about two horses who could run fast?"
Without a moment's lift of the head,
"No 'tory horses!"
came the uncapitulating reply.
I tried again: "Shall I tell you a story
about a nice man who had two little puppies?"
Again, with no less spirit and emphasis,
"No 'tory nice man!"

Then came an inspiration:
"Shall I tell you a story about Rachel?"
Now for the first time, the little head moved
and two eyes looked up: " 'tory Rechu?"
The bait was just too good,
and the little mourner was caught
in the net of excitement and self-interest.

I've wondered since,
may it not be that we've told too many stories
about horses that can run fast,
and nice men with puppies,
and have often forgotten to put
the Rachels and Richards, the Tommys and Trudys,
in the middle of the situation?
The cry for relevance is an early cry.

All Flights Cancelled

"All flights cancelled;
the airport is now closed."

Snowbound in an airport,
sixteen of us, wanting to be in Portland.
No longer strangers,
but one in a common frustration
and disappointment.
No longer in charge,
our psyches wounded and unwilling
to acknowledge complete dependence,
we struggle, we resist—
lash out in mutual anger
at falling into others' hands.

"They," we say, "they
can't do this to us!"
But they can, they do,
they've done it—
the invisible "they."

But one among us,
one small person,
roams free.

With so much to celebrate,
so much carpet and color,
and so much coordination,
he runs and rolls and jumps;
he sings, he shouts,
and in his smiles and songs
we find our solace.

Is it always so—
the spirit of the child within
leading us to relinquish ourselves
into strong, invisible hands—
hands which sustain all flights
and hold us in that hour of hours
when the word is stark and stern:
all flights cancelled?

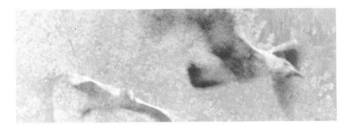

Science Lecture

I held her warm hand
as we walked in the park
at sunset, by the lake.

My mind recorded
her kindergarten lecture
as she chattered on:
"See the 'flections?
That's the fishes' world.
And do you know?
The sun is always shining
and the night is always nighting,
because, you see,
the world is round!"

I've paid tuition for less.

God's Kindergarten

Some day we'll see
that this spinning world
is one vast day-care center,
God's kindergarten, our home
away from Home.

Then we will know
that God has no grown-up children here,
but toddlers all, and blunderers,
failing, falling, stumbling,
picked up to try again, tripping,
always tripping over many things
that make us fall, but mostly
just our own two feet.

Let's Play Baptism

One little girl—
but that's changed now,
for she's big sister to a new baby.

It's been a busy time,
her mother said,
welcoming the new one,
preparing for the Baptism
and answering all the questions
of the three-year-old.

A snippet of conversation
with a nursery friend
startles her mother:
"Let's play Baptism.
I'll be God."

Oh, holy rashness
when innocence consults with no one
but the Spirit
and claims its birthright!

The Difference

He'd just received a box of crayons,
a birthday gift. Deluxe, it was,
with more than seventy colors,
and he was proud.

Whenever he found an audience
he'd empty every crayon out,
then separate the color families,
extolling the beauties of each.
Once, when the process ended,
he surprised a viewer
by reaching for one special crayon—
the periwinkle blue—
and saying, as he held it high,
"And this one is so pretty
it makes my eyes wet!"

He didn't say, "It makes me cry."
Young as he was, he knew the difference
between grief and encounter with
transcendence.

What readiness to be touched by the intangible,
what openness to beauty and to God!

Heaven

"Father, into your hands
I commit my spirit. . . ."
Luke 23:46

She held her father's hand
as they boarded the west-flying plane,
skipping along the carpeted ramp,
her feet hardly touching the floor.

"Where are we going?" he asked her
affectionately. "To Grandma's!"
was her instant reply.

She didn't say: To Bozeman
or Billings or Portland.
She saw a face,
not a place.

"Father," he said.
He too saw a Face.

In dying he found his way
home: "Into your hands,
your future, your presence
I commit my spirit." Perhaps
heaven isn't a place
but a Face.

We Have

Little sisters, four and six;
today the mail brought
what they liked and looked for,
a catalogue, replete with
many colored pictures.

The first to page it
was the six-year-old;
she turned each page possessively,
saying wherever she found what pleased her,
"I want this! And I want this . . . and this!"

The litany of selfishness ended,
came the moment of the four-year-old.
She, who didn't know the why of catalogues,
turned pages, pointing too,
but now the words were new:
"We got this! And we got this . . . and this!"

"I want!" "We have!" What difference
it would make in this, our global village,
if four-year-old love and wisdom ruled the day!

Friends

Four-year-old Chad,
to his devoted grandmother:
"I like it here, Grandma!"
"Why?" came the eager response.
"Because nobody hollers."
Then, quickly, he added,
"But Mom is more fun than you;
she can stand on her head."

One to bring serenity,
another hilarity,
each at the moment's demand.
Such is the vocation of family,
being, not all things to all,
but ripe with the seasons of friendship,
for without friendship
what is love?

Boxed In

She colored a giraffe today,
one ear pink, the other green,
a tail of blue, the body brown
with spots of many colors.

She brought her joyful offering
into the world of grown-ups,
and the first to see it said,
"But no one has ever seen
a giraffe like that!"
"Isn't that too bad!" was all she said.

Keep resisting, child,
those little boxes,
the cramped and stuffy judgments
that bury one alive.
Fight the brave battle
to be the one you are.

Innocence

What do they talk about
in the councils of the innocent,
where guru and disciples
are just four years old
and the big kids are in school?

What classic infant heresies
and learned theories are propounded,
what sovereign warnings spoken and comforts shared,
where the dogma of the playground
is proclaimed?

Wouldn't we really like to know,
we who've left it all behind?

The Threat

"And I'll skip you
in my prayers!"

The years have flown
since I overheard that tearful threat
from one who couldn't match
five years against the strength
and cunning of his older sibling.

Now there is the empty nest,
and I reflect on what that outcry meant:
a last resort, a final stand.
And now he is a man.

How large his world today,
how raw and sharp its edges.
Does he, I ask myself, now count prayer
as something to be treasured,
ultimate and priceless,
and will he always?

I bow my head.

The Demon Self-Doubt

He'd had a great year
in kindergarten,
but now the going was hard
in first grade.
After reflection and brooding,
he came to his mother with a sad self-assessment
and solemn conclusion:
"I don't think I'm really first grade;
I'm more kindergarten type."

For another, it had been a significant career,
fifty-five years of hard
and responsible work.
But now he sat alone,
downcast and discouraged.
As I approached him with a greeting he said:
"I'm no good; I can't work at anything any more."

Two persons,
each with a given dignity
and "justified by faith,"
both deep in self-evaluation
and suffering
at the hands of the demon, Self-Doubt,
both at a crossroad
and needing wise and compassionate friends.

Voices are needed,
my voice and yours,
voices of self-appointed guardians
of the fragile egos
of the very young and very old,
and everyone between,
voices to proclaim
that God has loved us
into dignity and worth forever.

One Race

Her first day of school,
its first of integration.
Her mother, apprehensive,
worked through the worrisome hours,
then ran to meet the school bus
in mid-afternoon.

"How did it go?" she cautiously enquired.
"Well, I sat next to a friendly little girl."
And now the daring question, the one
she feared to ask: "Was she . . . was she black?"
"Yes."
"And what happened? Tell me all about it."
"Oh, nothing. We were both so scared
we held hands all day."

Our best teachers—our children—teach us:
there is but one race, the human.
If we could only feel it,
sharers of many dreams and one destiny,
we'd be holding hands all day.

Treasure the Child

Grandma knew this was the awaited day,
one of the best in every year:
Christmas tree-trimming day in the home
of her small grandchild.
So she telephoned across town.

The buoyant voice answered,
and eagerly teased, "I'll bet
you don't know what we've got here!"
"Could it be a Christmas tree?"
was Grandma's knowing reply.
"Uh huh—do you want to talk to it?"

Talking trees or talked-to trees,
it's all the same when you're young in heart.
Treasure the child within and around you,
the free imagination and blithe spirit;
they warm the winter nights of memory.

Small Talk

"Granddaddy,
how did you marry Grandma?"
"Oh, I became acquainted with her
and I loved her right away."
"Was she pretty?"
"Oh, yes!"

"Did she have light hair?"
"No, very, very dark. And she was
graceful.
But Rachel, you are pretty too,
and you are graceful."
"Granddaddy, you don't have to
say that."
"I know I don't."
"You don't have to say it for my feelings."
"I know. I wouldn't say it
if it weren't true."

The child probes, tests, checks,
already searching for integrity and honesty
in society's tangle of flattery and lies.

Small talk?
Who could call it that?

Christmas Lesson

Christmas Eve,
everything in highest key,
the dinner, the tree, the songs and gifts;
but now the hour was late,
with only grown-ups left.
But then the best of all,
that round of visits to all four beds,
the ritual Christmas Eve inventory.

There he lay,
our child of seven Christmases,
dreams of celebration
reflected on his happy face.

But what was this,
protruding from the blanket?
Two new gloves—with rabbit fur, no less!

Soundly he slept in these,
his newest gifts.

"You teach us well, my son,"
I thought, "teach me, your grown-up dad,
(too big for grace sometimes),
the Christmas lesson: how gifts
are believed, received, possessed.
I salute you, child,
you great receiver from our Father's hand."

The Best Talk

"Do you know what we did?
We walked, and we had the best talk!"

Our eight-year-old granddaughter's
report to her grandmother.

My version:
It began with a lopsided question
as we walked, hand in hand.
"Granddaddy, do you really love me
more than anybody?"

My reply:
"Well, dear, it's like this:
I love Grandma most because she's my darling wife;
I love your mommy most because she's our eldest daughter;
I love her sister most because she's our middle daughter
and their sister most because she's our youngest daughter;
and then I love your uncle most because he's our only son.
Yes, and I love you most because you're our only granddaughter.
Love, you see, can handle lots of 'mosts.' "

To you and me, hardly worth the telling;
but to her, "the best talk"—another "most"!

Be Kind

"You know, Mom,
your world is pretty nice
compared to going out to recess."

Startling words from one
in fourth grade;
they surprised her mother
as they do me.
They tell us that we
can't see clearly
the "worlds" of one another,
that threatening things
appear so tame when
faced by someone else.

They tell us, too,
to look and listen.
They say: "Be kind."

Child Wisdom

I couldn't suppress a smile
when she, the ten-year-old,
shared a self-searching moment:
"I don't know what I'm going to do
with my life; there are so many things
I'm interested in, but I've already
invested ten years in art."

Today I thank that wistful child
who spoke more wisely than she knew.

God dreams his dream for me,
enlists me for the full-time task of moving on.
My life is a becoming;
he will not let me be.
There's no rehearsal for the art of living;
no vacation from the journeying.

It all begins with his first gift—
day one!

Thresholds

Essay time in the sixth
grade composition class, and the
subject was assigned: "Things I Hate."

With pencil-chewing,
hair rumpling, and a good bit
of paper-crumpling, she
of eleven summers, wrote:
"I've thought and thought,
but I guess I don't hate anything
except boys, not men, just boys.
I don't think I really hate boys,
they just bother me; I know that
I'm going to have to get used to
them, and I just hope I do soon
because I know some real cute ones."

We cross strange, mysterious
thresholds in life's journey, and
encounter sharp corners. We're
catapulted from stage to stage
from Who-am-I? to
Who-am-I-to-you?

Wow!

Thank God for "Wow!"
that boisterous exclamation point
when there's nothing more
to say.

Cherries

"You know, life isn't
just a bowl of cherries."
I said it to my granddaughter.
"No," she flashed back, "sometimes it's
just a bunch of ants!"

She said it well.
Life can be a long procession
of pesky irritations, too small to count.

But thank God still for the cherries;
the night-time breeze that moves through
rustling leaves, the healing touch or
fleeting smile, and the still, small voice.
God hides his majesty in these.

Swaying Room

Today I have been tutored
by the forest in its wisdom.

One week ago I cut some aspens into post lengths,
reverting to my farmer days.
(I'll cut them for the fireplace
some other time, I told myself.)
I placed them tip to tip around a growing tree.
Today that sturdy tree is broken,
shattered eight feet above the ground.

I killed the tree by forcing it
to be more rigid than any growing thing can be—
a thoughtless thing to do.
I should have known
that living things need swaying room;
it's also true of persons.

Yes, growing things need space,
room for changing and responding.
Brittle systems maim and kill.

Just Think

The big examination was over
in the sixth-grade civics class.
That night she added this to her
usual bedtime prayer: "And please, God,
make Omaha the capital of Nebraska. Amen."

But think, my child, just think:
If God would send a statehouse
winging on one child's troubled prayer,
and change your grade from B to A—
yes, if God placed us in a world like that—
think of all the frightened people
in the statehouse, and all the perfect papers,
unemployed teachers, confused preachers,
stationary rivers, tropical shivers,
and the infinite, magic mess!

Love Cheats

I remember my mouthy days,
my dazzling debates
with Mom and Dad.

Like a winner,
confidently I'd argue,
condescendingly I'd instruct,
tolerantly I'd repeat,
patiently I'd wait,
until, without a moment's warning,
one of them would say,
"You know, we love you!"

"Foul!" I'd yearn to cry,
and I'd want out.
They'd struck so hard—
and below the belt.

Love cheats.
It always does;
there's no defense.

Jubilee

"I'm confirmed!"
She called out to me,
almost shouted, right in the
chancel of the church; said it
with a hop and a skip, and a flounce
of her long white robe.

How unbecoming, one might say;
how unfitting!—leave jubilee
to angels.

I see it now as most becoming,
for what better reason to celebrate?
And why not with timbrel and dance!

Do You Remember?

Do you remember when your parents
became a problem to you?
They'd left you with careful instructions,
but you overstepped their lines,
and you weren't pleased to see them
come home.

You worked out your scheme,
your thin little stratagems
to outwit them, but you were first found,
then quickly found out.

Today the problem may be like that
with God. Has he become an intruder,
not welcome at all?

Gone are the fours, the fives, the sixes—
the children's sizes, but the shoes
point away—from God, I mean.
But thank God he's God. He's not trail-tired.
He finds us out,
and finds us.

This Land of Leaving

The curly-tailed colt,
the velvet-nosed one—
what perfect days he had,
shadowing his mother,
no waiting, no worrying,
every meal on time.

Then came the day:
"We must wean him," Father said.
"This is the time."

We watched the shock
as the big gate closed,
listened to the frenzy,
suffered in his search.

"Den förste sorg," my father sighed.
("The first sorrow.")

I think of this today
in this land of leaving,
a place of weaning;
I feel it, too, and so do you;
one fact fringes all.

We Won

I remember a moment long ago
in a small-town restaurant.

We'd played a basketball game—
played away from home and won,
and were in a celebrative mood.
I was fourteen, and not very good,
nor was our team, and this made victory
sweeter still.

As we crowded into a booth
I jauntily said, "Well, we won!"
Quick as the flash of a knife
came the remembered words:
"What do you mean, 'we'?
You didn't play!"

I can't forget the words
or the one who spoke them,
but I can turn to other words,
sounding in my soul.
My Lord says, "This do
in remembrance of me."
Baptized into the death of Christ
I die in him to rise again.
With no part in the victory
I'm still invited to say,
"We won!"

Family Talk

It takes the whole church
to say "Jesus,"
and when all have said it,
you in your way
and I in mine,
what do we have?
Orchestrated understatement.

Our best dogma
of spoken creed
or faithful deed
is but the insufficient
baby talk of us,
the family of God.

Yet he,
our Father,
takes pleasure
and listens patiently
to our lisping growth.

Where Thought Breaks Down

"You know, we're here."
"Yeah, we exist.
Isn't that something?"

Overheard from a conversation
of two eighteen-year-olds
as they painted our house
(they didn't know).

Only the smallest snippet,
nothing more, but enough,
enough to set us all
to pondering the poignancy
of the fact
that we *are!*

We may go further,
but we can't go deeper,
for it brings us
straight to the A
of the alphabet of mystery,
the "In the beginning God" moment,
where thought breaks down
and yields to prayer.

Make Room

When did it happen
that he gained a stride on me
and shouldered the heavier load?

I saw him born.
Was it then
that he signaled from afar
the classic sign, where a generation
crosses over, cries for space
and room to be?

Is this what the first cry means:
"I'm here! Make room for me!"?
The beauty and the pain of one
bright hour,
like the rising and the falling
of a star.

Summer

Loose-Leaf

When your options are either
to revise your beliefs
or to reject a person,
look again.

Any formula for living
that is too cramped
for the human situation
cries for re-thinking.

Hard-cover catechisms
are a contradiction
to our loose-leaf lives.

One Generation to Another

"One generation shall laud thy works to another,
and shall declare thy mighty acts."
Psalm 145:4

Kabekona. Magic word.
To me, two decades of family,
a clear, blue lake,
and a woodland cabin;
more than twenty babies
(cousins in the clan),
"leaving father and mother,"
always to return to this place held dear.

When I think of Kabekona
I remember
the words of one of the cousins,
now eighteen years old.
Addressing his aunt, he asked,
"Do you know what I like best about Kabekona?"
"No, what?" she answered.
"We're all in the same room!" he said.

"All in the same room."
An exciting description of education
as cross-generational sharing,
hearing and telling old family stories
which flow into the Story, older still.

Making Love

Making love,
the ultimate frolic,
is the art of being second;
you dare not be good to yourself
until you've been good to the other.

Nourished, and sometimes saved, by a sense of humor,
love is the horizon of all that's human,
forever beyond our grasp, never fully attained.

Our Mystery

She?
She loved
the pilgrim soul
in me.

The journey seemed right
to both of us,
so natural,
—that's our shared mystery!

Love Talk

In a sober moment
I am reminded of this thought:
Nothing good is ever cheap.

Love talk is like
opening a charge account.
First you learn the words,
then you learn the price,
and finally you pay it.

God's Way for Me

The profoundest thing
one can say of a river
is that it is on its way to the sea.

The deepest thought
one can think of persons
is that they are citizens of eternity.

Moments and years,
years and moments,
pass like sea-bent streams.
And I? I'm carried on the current
of an all-possessing love.
I'm on my way, God's way for me,
so let it be.

To Be a Friend

Only yesterday
she startled me
by saying, "Dad,
you'll never understand me."
"Why?" I gulped; she said:
"Not because you're not
an understanding person,
but you've never been single!"

Never been, never been!
Oh, yes, I'd been single—
but never out of school.
So she was right.

God, I've taken pride in
instant understanding,
I, who live with so
many "never beens."
Help me to know that I'm locked out
of much that really matters,
to show respect for others' secrets,
to be a friend on the doorsteps
of those whom I love.

The Challenge

"You shouldn't have come today,
because now you are the people
who know."

I felt singled out that day,
twenty-five years ago. I still do.

We had assembled in a new science facility
to dedicate and enjoy and to listen
to a scholar in the field of genetics,
and those were his closing words.
Bracing, compelling, personal—
the words still fill me
with the peril and promise
of things known and understood.

Closing words that day, but opening, too,
for they are a challenge, a reminder
that all new knowledge involves one
in greater responsibility and urgent choice.

My Personal Devil

My personal devil
is passionately in favor of the good
as long as it keeps me from the Best.
He seldom deals in blacks and whites,
but loves the many shades of gray;
he likes options, and offers many.
He keeps the lines blurred.

His art is to distract.

Lord, Help Me

Forgive my absences, Lord,
and help me not to
miss so much.

School me in the full stop
and the long look,
lest I miss your kind approaches.

Tune me to echoes and undertones;
make me alive to foretastes
and afterglows.

Awaken me to your heralds
and harbingers, wherever
I am. Amen.

The Lived Life

I remember a little pair of shoes.
For months they stood side by side
on the closet floor,
begging for feet.

We had an active four-year-old
who ran and danced through the days
with always new plans for the morrow.
But one day she lay still
in a distant hospital
while the weeks went by.
It was polio.

We had shopped for shoes
and she loved hers especially
because they were her first that tied.
I remember praying,
as we put them aside,
that they would be worn again.

That experience taught me
that it is high privilege
to support life.
Never since have I complained
about the price of children's shoes.

Life is meant to beget and sustain more life.
To grow tired is not tragedy
if one is living by loving,
dying by giving.

The call to discipleship
is to "come and die,"
usually not in one burst of effort
nor in a single pool of blood,
but in the steady self-draining
of life-strength and energy.

There's no room for self-pity
in the lived life.
Only the unlived quality
of our existence
should ever make us sad.

Home

Home is where you are
even when you're not;
where you unbutton whatever is pinching you,
loosen whatever is choking you,
set down whatever is breaking you,
and tell whatever is bothering you.

Home is where someone is expecting you,
where your chair, your plate,
your bed are always kept for you,
where a memory, a plan, a dream, a laugh
or a tear is freely shared with you.

Home is where you let up and let down,
where you stop hiding and let yourself be found,
where you quit being someone else
and are just your needy old self.

A Dirty Word

"No person is ever merely to be
tolerated; it is more humane
to attack."

These words heard at a convocation
put me in mind of more familiar words
from our little ethnic ghetto where I was shaped;
words urging us to exercise religious, racial,
social, and every other sort of toleration.

Who am I to play God,
granting my permission
to my sister and my brother
to exist, to be?

Now I see in *tolerance*
a dirty word.

Soggy Cereal and Tepid Tea

When I remember that I am a parent,
and think of God as Father,
I recall a special breakfast
brought to me in bed.

We awoke early
to the sound of hurrying feet.
We wondered what they were up to,
our four- and eight-year-olds;
but soon it came—
breakfast in bed.

It was an elaborate menu:
chilled burnt toast, with peanut butter;
eggs, fried, and chilled too;
soggy cereal,
(the milk had been added too soon)
and tepid tea.
A horrendous mix.

When they stepped out for a moment
to get something they'd forgotten (heaven forbid!)
my wife whispered,
"You're going to have to eat this, I can't!"
And I did.

I didn't eat as a gourmet,
for it wasn't gourmet cooking;
I didn't even eat as a hungry man
for I wasn't hungry.

I ate it as a father
because it was made for me;
I was expected to:
they had faith in me.
And I ate because it was served on eager feet
and with starry eyes.

I think of my poor service to God
as teacher, parent,
interpreter of the Good News.
I know that my offerings are soggy,
tepid and unfit,
but my Father receives them
and even blesses them—
not because I am good
but because he is!

The Goal

In parenting and teaching,
let this be our aim:
not to make every idea
safe for children, but
every child safe
for ideas.

One More

Teacher,
when you've worked hard
and nothing happens,
when you've prepared well
but nothing comes off,
when every thought
crashes on the runway
and the whole lesson trails on the ground—
then, don't forget
to count One more than
you can see!

Homecoming

"Father, I have sinned . . .
I am no longer worthy. . . ."
Luke 15:18

He had rehearsed it well.
The hills didn't interrupt,
and the swine went on with
their eating
as is their habit.

Now the road bends, the prodigal is home,
the Father is in sight.
Two deep breaths, and a sigh:
"Father, I have sinned—
against heaven and before you;
I am no more worthy to be called
your son. . . ."

But the Father hears no more.
Love-deafened, he takes charge
and fills the air
with party talk.

The Father is like that;
he interrupts the confession
with celebration.

I Am Found

"No one shows a child the sky."
The African proverb halts me,
breaks my stride and reminds me
that some things don't need heralding.
They compel by being there.
Like God, they find me.

We Live on Glimpses

We live on glimpses,
fleeting glimpses in the forest;
this is its beauty,
this its charm.

A bit of furry fluff
disappearing behind a log,
the flash of a many-colored wing
telling us that a bird is hiding in the bush.
Wild things always in flight,
leaving us wishing for more,
more time to examine and admire,
more to hold in the hand.

We live on glimpses and wish for time-exposures;
but perhaps this is best:
to see wild things in the open,
untamed and free,
not caged or constrained, but free to go away.
For beauties are enhanced when they are fleeting;
they leave us hungry still.

We live on glimpses of great truths,
wild truths, like the fact of God's saving love.
To teach is never to tame or domesticate;
it is to acquaint each other
with truth on the wing,
unpredictable, unmanageable,
truth that seeks and seizes,
and will not be captured or contained.

Frightened

I'm always frightened
when I see strident arrogance
walk the streets,
especially in one I love,
for I know that sorrow
walks close behind.

Made in God's Image

No one ever quite
knows another,
no matter how close
they may be.

There is more
to me than what you see;
it comes with the image—
the image of God.

How Comforting

This morning our white-robed pastor startled us.
"I've been asked to announce," he said,
"that there's a blue pick-up in the parking lot
with its lights on. . . .
'Let us pray for the whole people of God.' "

He should have paused, perhaps,
but inadvertently he proclaimed to us
that God, in his vast providence,
runs it altogether too.
The God of this global village
is mindful of his children on the parking lot.

How comforting to know that he who watches
over galaxies and infinite expanses in his created world
notes too the two-for-a-penny sparrow's fall;
he keeps tabs on us, his absent-minded ones,
who are always forgetting to turn off the lights.

Alive Again

Today I left the freeway
to meander and explore,
experience the winding sideroads,
and I'm a person again.

On the freeways of the mind
generalizations hurry by,
and amid stampeding statistics,
person starves for person.
Crowding, nudging, jostling,
there's little touching
and not much meeting there.

I thank God for freeways—
my world is bigger now—
but I'll not do my living there.
Solitude demands friendship,
lest it turn to loneliness
and make one callous
to man's inhumanity to man.

Now I treasure the "asides,"
the little country roads
where I slow down
and let the other person in.

Only Sometimes

Faith is a frightened bird,
perched high.

Unwilling to abandon,
and waiting to return—
never out of sight
of its heart-home—
it waits in trembling trust,
often silent, but sometimes,
only sometimes, with a song!

Only Visiting

Five in the morning,
sunrise in Minnesota's lakeland.
At this moment the world
is burnished gold.

I stand alone at the cabin window
in solitary enjoyment
of midsummer sights and sounds.
Alone? No, not alone, for he is here,
the little half-grown chipmunk;
he's celebrating the sun,
blinking, rolling, stretching,
awakening every tiny nerve and muscle,
readying himself for the new day.

And she is here, the summer warbler,
and the hummingbirds,
both master and mistress.
Alone? No, never.
More eyes than I can count are on me
as I sit quietly.

One and all they look me over,
citizens of this diverse community,
startled, surprised, curious
and just a bit indignant.
They make me quite defensive.

"You, trespassing again?" they seem to say.
"I thought I owned this land," is my embarrassed answer.
"I hold the title. I've paid!"
But it's not clear to them—or me.
These are the rightful owners. They live here.
I don't belong. I'm only visiting. I'm the intruder;
my deed is dated; theirs is dateless and supreme.

What is ownership among us mortals, anyway?

Earth's Cry

"God blessed them, . . . 'Be fruitful,
and multiply, and fill the earth
and subdue it.' "
Genesis 1:28a

Seldom in time
has earth's cry
been so plaintive;
the rapist's spirit
is abroad.

Earth fears our greedy hearts
and ruthless hands.

When will we honor the voice that says
to subdue is not to plunder,
but to woo.

The Movement of Grace

Like ocean waves,
beating against wet rocks
and washing miles of shore,
so the "blesseds" bear in upon me.
In them God's mercy comes,
and always there's more!
This is the movement of grace,
always toward me.
The inheritance seeks the heir.

It is a loving plan,
God's plan for me,
his purpose to pursue.
I run after the good,
but the best runs after me.
The Hound of Heaven is on my trail.
(I hear the "blesseds,"
and in them the baying of the Hound.)

"The only thing there's enough of,"
and it seeks me,
not *it,* but *he;*
He seeks me; a gracious plan.
Even so, come, Lord Jesus.

Idolatry

If the full and final answer
could once be spied and grasped,
we'd melt it down and settle in
and have a golden calf.

The God who knows
asks us to love our incompleteness
—that saving gift that keeps us
in the quest.

Forgiveness

As a struggling writer,
I have a thing about mistakes.
Whenever I make one
no crude correction will do.
I must put the blemish behind me;
I need a new page.

So with each evening and morning,
the old day and the new.
We can't be content with Band-aids;
we cry for a new creation
—for forgiveness and starting over.

A Lesson

Today I learned a lesson,
the simplest kind of lesson—
from a fruit jar cover.

My first turn was wrong;
but I was stubborn,
and I was strong.

The second was more wrong
because I was strong.

And now it sticks.

How sad to be strong
(and stubborn)
when you're wrong!

Our Lord Says, "Go!"

Our Lord says, "Go!"
and we take an opinion poll
or make another survey.

Our Lord says, "Go!"
and we rewrite constitutions
and study bylaws.

Our Lord says, "Go!"
and we fill out forms
in triplicate and blue and green.

Our Lord says, "Go!"
and we reorganize
what we just overorganized.

Our Lord says, "Go!"
and we volunteer for committees
or join discussion groups.

We know the words, but we don't dare.
We don't say yes, we don't say no, we temporize;
we don't refuse, we procrastinate,
all with the rhetoric of love.

Our Lord still says, "Go!"

The Way We Turn

The way we turn at parting
for one last look or smile,
one lingering gesture of devotion
from those we love—
does it signal something
from beyond?

Is it, perhaps, our concession to
mortality?

Why

Why is the hurting word,
the ennobling word. No one can
hold back *why* any more than we hold
our breath. It will be asked.

But there are many ways of asking.
We can curse it, snarl it,
pout or cry or whimper. We can also pray.
God waits for us to pray the question,
Why?

Let Us Give Thanks

Let us give thanks this moment:
for the sturdy fact of God's continuing love,
for mercies which go before us
and follow after us,
for those free gifts
which cost God so much.

Let us give thanks:
for memory and expectation,
for the good that we have known
and know today in Jesus Christ,
for the Spirit's brooding presence
in our nights and in our days.

Let us give thanks:
for pleasures which comfort
and pains which force our growth
and keep us at the Shepherd's side,
for deep meanings revealed
and mysteries mercifully concealed,
for the image of God within us,
the capacity to inquire and adore.

Let us give thanks for one another,
for just being together,
for differences which complement and complete,
for gifts which enrich
and disagreements which challenge,
for our oneness in Christ.

Let us give thanks for melody and mirth,
for rhythm and beat,
for the repeated and the common,
for the ever-unfolding,
and for senses with which to respond.

And let us give thanks for Someone to thank.

Disguise

Someone said that it requires much courage
to walk into a room full
of human beings and be human.

I am reminded of a Halloween party
we had missed.

"How was the party?" we asked
of one who'd been there.
"Oh, fine," he answered,
"Everyone came masked
and dressed like someone else,
and then there was a Saint Bernard;
he came as a dog."

Noble beast;
no mask, no wall,
no camouflage.
He came as himself.
To him the prize!

Autumn

I'm Glad

"Does the road wind
uphill all the way?"
"Yes, to the very end,"
writes Christina Rosetti.

The right road winds,
and uphill, too;
there are few lazy stretches,
no coasting places.

They didn't tell me that,
or maybe I wasn't listening.
Oh, I expected some hard times—
a slip and a loss now and then,
but nothing I couldn't regain.
I thought I'd be in control.

Today I see.
I know.

I've savored joy,
but I also know the great peace
that comes with an accepted sorrow.
And I'm glad the control
is not left to me.

I Understand

I used to think
that imagination
is just for "tripping,"
going places, wild places,
meeting people, wild people,
and for setting goals.

Now I understand
that imagination
is for *loving,*
for wearing others' shoes,
getting into others' skins.

How can one care
if one can't imagine,
can't see and feel
from the other side?

Imagination is for caring,
serving, helping with the invisible load.
Imagination, the mind's pleasure cruise,
but the heart's workroom.

Everything Is Different

"And behold, angels came
and ministered to him."

Angels came.
Our Lord experienced this,
and my heart says, "Me, too!"

Nothing has changed,
yet everything is different
(don't ask me to explain):
My journey waits, my cross remains,
my wilderness retains its wildness.
But, oh, the difference
since angels came!

Rejoice with Me

"And the Pharisees and the scribes
murmured, saying, 'This man receives sinners
and eats with them.' "
Luke 15:2

They just stood there,
missing the point of the best
that has ever happened.

Their sullen, straightlaced slander,
"He receives sinners," was really
highest praise.

In their blindness
they thought to protect him,
concerned lest his righteousness
prove too fragile to risk
contact with the unclean.

"Receives sinners!"—bad enough—
but "even eats with them!"
The good people were sure
that something must be done.
Muttering into their beards,
they gathered in knots,
discussed a lot and argued some,
did everything but ask him
what this really meant.

But he spoke to all:
Your artificial correctness
makes you hard of hearing;
your concern over trivia
robs you of your joy.

Rejoice with me at every human response,
be open to newness,
and don't forget to be glad.

Jesus used a story,
the one about the ninety-and-nine,
aimed it at their hearts
and didn't miss.

Sunrise

"The steadfast love of the Lord
never ceases, his mercies . . .
are new every morning."
Lamentations 3:22-23

Some things most worth knowing
can never be fully, finally learned.
I need reminders every day,
tutors to hold me
to my ABCs.

It dawned on me today,
the steady proclamation
that eternal life begins with faith,
not death.

I needn't wait to die
before I begin to live;
this very day I go to meet my heaven.
My Lord has come—is coming—to me
in the mercies of God,
new every morning.

'Tis sunrise to my soul.

Maturity

Our little maple,
just four feet tall two years ago,
but today I first saw a bird
perch briefly
among her branches.

So now our tree is more than a tree;
she is connected, she has reached out,
offered herself to a universe of needs.
She's promise, shelter, resting place;
she offers habitat.

So with us too, the family
of humankind.
We're meant to offer homes
to one another
as confidants and burden-sharers.
This is maturity.

To the Perpetual Critic

Please tell me, Sir or Madam:
how you can expect
to find a little of the best
in the worst, when you've spent yourself
in looking for a little of the worst
in the best?

Dead

"No time for sunsets,"
I heard him say, that most efficient man.

No time to reach beyond
the arm's short grasp,
just time to measure, weigh and count,
to rush past messages and meanings,
to seek the living among the dead.

I've Begun Asking

I'm breaking my habit
of asking strangers,
"What do you do?"
as if they're no more than what they do.

I've begun asking,
"What are your dreams and your dreads?
What moves you, excites you, alarms you?
What drains you or sustains you?
What interests or bores you, amuses or grieves you?
Where do you go when you're homesick?
Where do you rest when you're tired?
Who are you when you're alone, and whom do you miss?
And who misses you?"

But when we're dealing with questions,
perhaps it's really not what or where or who,
but *whose*. Whose are you? And whose am I?

Prayer

"Be still, and know that I am God."
Psalm 46:10

Prayer?
What is it
but letting God be God,
letting him love you in your being
and in your becoming?

Prayer.
The stillness you know
when you wait because
you know Who waits
for you.

Knowledge

Knowledge without faith
is only baggage;
it weighs the traveler down.

But knowledge that believes
gains two wings. It soars.

Faith-winged,
it greets the depths with joy,
flying over deep, deep valleys
of things unknown.

It breathes mountain air.

Zero

There's "nothing I wouldn't do for you,"
and "nothing you wouldn't do for me,"
so we don't do a thing for one another.

"Let's get together some time," we say.
"Yes, come and visit me;
drop by when you're in the neighborhood."
Without specific response
to particular need,
vague good intentions become
an easy exit
into the never-never land
of callous fantasy.

And I become a
bloodless, voiceless, careless zero,
never really harming anyone,
just leaving them to die alone.

Can This Be?

Where life is all
one gentle slope,
a vast, uninterrupted drift
with nothing that needs doing,
and one's full-time project
is to please oneself—
no milestones, nothing to punctuate—
can this be it . . .
can this be hell?

I Met a Man

I met a man this wintry morning.
Stooping to pull on my overshoes,
I looked up, and there he was.

I greeted him with a hello;
he greeted me as pleasantly,
but hello was all he said.

That is all;
hardly worth the telling
in this world of large events,
and yet enough to call forth the question in me:
What do I really know of this young man?

I don't know his name,
his date or place of birth,
his family, friends or home address.
I can't guess what's on his mind or in his heart,
or where he's been or where he's going.
And yet, I know he's born and didn't ask to be;
and he will die, but doesn't want to.

I know too, with knowledge born of faith,
that he is loved and wanted
in the highest heaven.

One thing more I know:
He's lonely.
Like me, he knows much more than he can tell,
has feelings he cannot fully share.

These universals bind us all together;
we share the wonder and the pain of being;
we know its source and sense a Presence.
This we know of one another.

"I've Missed You"

I knocked today at my friend's door;
he answered, and I went in.
"I've the best possible reason
for coming," I said.
"What's that?" said he.
"I've missed you."

I had no other reason.
I just wanted to stand up close,
shoulder to shoulder, heart to heart,
with this, my friend.
We found it reason enough.

What Shall I Say?

What shall I say when they come,
my sister, my brother in distress,
I who am mortal, and so fallible too?

Shall I say,
"Take a trip to the Grand Tetons,
stop by their snow-fed streams,
drink like a breast-fed babe
and try to taste God?"

Or
"Hold a puppy in your lap
and stroke its silken ears?"

No, not these footnotes,
grace-filled as they may be.
I'll invite them to the
headline—the Name:
"Jesus-Emanuel (God with us)!
Whisper it, shout it, pray it.
Yes, cry it, cry out against it
if you must, but test it,
taste it, experience how true it is,
how tough and how tender.

"Yes, come to him!"
That's what I'll say.

I Wasn't Ready

"Jerry died this evening," a soft voice said,
as I answered the call of the telephone.

Jerry, my friend and fellow explorer,
select among many, for we had taken trips together.
We'd journeyed far while staying right at home;
traveled, not by plane and train,
but from thought to thought.
We had soared on wings of mystery, and words like these:
"I wonder, can it possibly be . . . ?"

"Jerry died. . . ."
I'd known for weeks such words would come,
but I wasn't ready for the heavy thud
of word on word. One never is,
for the Spirit's readiness is God's to give,
offered in pace with need. It calls us
to ourselves and keeps us open.

Her Gift

She's a mother,
and worthy of the title.
Yesterday she shared a moment,
a hard one she'd experienced
with her beloved son.

"He's been depressed," she said,
"just not himself at all.
I tried to comfort him, but failed."
She paused, then added ruefully,
"I just broke down and cried;
I'd promised myself that I wouldn't,
but I did. Oh, I did suggest
that he read Romans 8, but then
I couldn't hold back my tears."

Failed? She drew him out, pointed
to the Source. Romans 8. She
couldn't have made a better choice.
And she cried.
How many persons in his life
have cared enough to cry?
She witnessed to God's love and hers;
did her best, and sealed it
with that costly gift—her tears.

Look Again

If you would live creatively,
look again at what God
has placed before you
but you have never fully seen:
a place, a situation, an idea,
a person, a face—especially the face
of one you love or hate,
of one you take for granted or ignore,
or one prejudged and now avoided.

There never was a human face
that wasn't worth another look.

Trusting

Our five birch trees are locked in icy embrace,
their branches bent almost to the ground.
I wonder, will they ever raise
again their weighted arms?

There are such winter moments
in a lifetime of faith
when no bird sings, heavy moments
of menacing despair.

But the birches will rise again
because they are birches.
So faith bends too but doesn't break,
for trusting One who is trustworthy
keeps faith from faltering
when no one can explain.

Our Distant Drummer

We are at odds
with the rhythms of living
as surely as we lose the throb
of the cosmic within
our souls.

From the beginning
God, the distant drummer,
set the tempo.

I'm the One
(To My Friends and Family)

I'm the one I never see;
my camera clicks, and they're all there
but me.

Imprisoned in myself,
I have a grandstand view
of all the faults and foibles
of everyone but me.

Perhaps I wouldn't like myself so well
if I could really see;
my thanks to all who love and like
in spite of all they see in me.

God's Shut-In

"God said to Noah,
'. . . I will establish my covenant
with you. . . .' "
Genesis 6:13, 18

We know the story,
how the storm clouds gathered,
thunder rolled, lightning flashed,
as Noah went in, into the ark,
the dark of the ark, where the Lord shut him in.

And it rained. And rained. And rained!

Noah waited, while the Lord remembered
his promise to Noah,
his shut-in.

It was hard to wait,
but the great day came
when Noah strode forth
into the blinding light
of God's promise.

My ark and me,
God's shut-in;
I wait and wonder,
but he, the Lord, remembers
while it rains.

Seven Seconds

Last evening,
in seven terrifying seconds
the tornado struck. Today all but one
of our eight trees are totally destroyed—
seven trees, seven familiar friends.

I'm reminded that five houses
can be built from one towering redwood,
but one redwood can't be built
from five houses.

That miracle belongs to God:
a seven-second lesson
in humility.

Diminished

He died today;
they sat him down alone,
alone in that cold chair,
strapped him to hopelessness
and dark despair.

Five men took aim.
They couldn't miss
and didn't.

We grope and fumble for a word
and call it justice
but are not satisfied.

Defeat, dead end for all of us,
mocks and shames, convicts, embarrasses,
leaves only leaden silence.

I look at you; you look at me;
we look away.

He died today; I am diminished,
and all humans with me. Have mercy, Lord,
on him, on me, on us, the sinners.

Thank You, Lord

Thank you, Lord,
for always answering prayer,
but not indulging
my every petty, private *give me*.
Thank you for winnowing and refining,
vetoing and delaying,
refusing and revising.

Thank you for being God
and never less,
for freeing me for wide horizons,
for protecting me from
my limited vision
and wayward will.

Thank you for foiling my every effort
to unseat you
and make myself king.
Thank you for keeping it safe
for me to pray.

A Simple Man

They say
he was a simple man
and sometimes walked
as in a dream.

But I remember what they said
about his dying child.
That just before
the last, long breath,
he, the simple man,
enfolded with a world of love
his dying one, and said,
"Are you all right?"
"Yes," came the faint reply,
"I'm not afraid to meet Jesus
if he's like you."

Love Knows

Never in the midst of mourning
does love regret its giving,
and one to another, weeping, say:
If only we'd given less to the one who died
we'd have more today.

Love knows the lie, and knowing,
rejoices in the spending.

Going On

In the long shadows of late November
we stood at the grave of one beloved
as husband, father, friend,
and I overheard soft-spoken words,
not meant for me,
but words to remember.

The moment had arrived,
that time that comes
in every hour of grief,
the moment for going on.
It was then that she,
the daughter and the only child,
spoke words intended just
for her mother: "Well, Mama?"

Two softly spoken words,
nothing more, and yet so much
in meaning and in courage,
much with which to turn together
toward a future with a different face,
words of hope and love, great love,
for we honor those who've taught us before parting
to face forward by going on.

Grounds for Hope

"The light shines in the darkness,
and the darkness has not overcome it."
John 1:5

If I am asked
what are my grounds for hope,
this is my answer:
Light is lord over darkness,
truth is lord over falsehood,
life is ever lord over death.

Of all the facts I daily live with,
there's none more comforting
than this: If I have two rooms,
one dark, the other light,
and I open the door between them,
the dark room becomes lighter
without the light one
becoming darker. I know
this is no headline,
but it's a marvelous footnote;
and God comforts me in that.

Worship

The Call to Worship:
You ask me why I heed this call
and let some other calls go by?
Let me try to answer.

Worship punctuates my page,
gives meaning to all it contains,
and addresses the "why" in my surfeited world
of "how-to's."

Worship replenishes my "therefore"
and reminds me of the great "because,"
the Cross of Jesus my Lord.

Worship lets me
sing my way
through constant change
and live joyfully
in the flow.

Worship provides a plot
to this otherwise incoherent
and senseless
world stage.

Whose Dream Am I?

I enjoy the moving picture from the highway:
mile on mile of theatre
and my own wandering mind.

Whose dream was this abandoned house?
Who laced the picture window?
Who chose the color, and when?
How old is old for a nourished dream,
a house, a home?

Who was the bride, and who the groom?
Did he carry her over the threshold?
Did they work and save and plan?
How many children played on this porch
when it was new?

My journey's over, and I'm home again.
I stand before the mirror.
Whose dream am I?
Who thought my life when it began?
Who shaped me in my mother's womb?
Who gives the years?
Who makes the days
and fills the moments?
Who holds the future?
Who says, "Enough"?

I hear his voice. He speaks to me:
"I don't abandon, for my dream
is you."

I Wasn't Afraid

"And I wasn't scairt—
I wasn't afraid to die!"

He said it as one who'd returned
from the outer spaces
in the journey of the soul.
And he had.

He said it as one who'd tasted
and tested, and settled something,
as one who'd been found
by the Father in a most
unfatherly place.
And he had.

It happened while he worked alone
in a city gravel pit.
A sudden collapse, a fall,
a tangle of cables,
and no one to hear his cries.
Two hours he hung, head down,
suffered in that forsaken place
until he was rescued,
but our Father found him there.

Another hung suspended,
alone upon his cross.
He cried to God, cried
in that most unfatherly place:
"My God, my God, why
have you forsaken me?
. . . Into thy hands
I commend my spirit."

And because he cried,
and prayed,
and died,
there is today no God-forsaken place,
or moment, or man,
or woman, or child—
no God-forsaken person anywhere.

Not afraid to die?
I need not cry,
but only pray,
"Father. . . ."

Joker

My mind is landlord to my thoughts;
I invite and entertain them.
But somehow vagrant thoughts move in,
and make their plans to stay.

I'm carried back
through many years of family fun
to a well-remembered joke.

We placed a birdhouse.
The day for leasing came.
The royal palace waited,
newly painted, nicely mounted,
right in size and every other way.

Proudly, haughtily, we waited
one day, three days, ten. No birds!
They didn't like us,
the empty birdhouse seemed to say.
We peered, we gazed, we stared.
One day it came. We had a tenant!
But what? But who?
Someone, something
looked out at us and then withdrew.
But who?

"Binoculars! Get the binoculars!" someone
said, and I was first in line.

I waited, waited for the movement
of the pretty little head,
that bright-eyed little songster
we wanted so to greet.

It came, I looked, I laughed!
I saw . . . a toad.

Today I thought an inappropriate thought.
Like a toad in a birdhouse it came,
and moved in as one who planned to stay.
I shooed it, threatened it, commanded it.
I laughed at it, and thought of that joker,
the toad.

Never Too Busy

This morning, very early,
I sensed the Spirit-Presence
stirring in my heart.
"May I come in?" the
Presence seemed to say,
and then it came.

We shared secrets,
mine from musty darkness,
the Spirit's from blinding light.
We spoke of many things,
of this day and tomorrow,
of joy and sorrow, life and life again.

We spoke of death—
my death.

Feeling my heart's tremor,
the Presence said,
"You needn't hurry;
my world can wait."
At last I stammered softly,
"But I still need your visits;
may we do this again?"
"I'm never too busy," the Spirit said.

Winter

I Hear a Voice

In these late years
I hear voices,
a cacophony
of shrill, familiar voices.

They say,
go faster, go farther,
climb higher, get more;
and don't forget:
more will make more,
and someday it'll
be most.

But then, above the din
I hear another voice:
No, go deeper, deeper
—deeper than that.

Just when it appears
that all gates close
and I'm running out of directions,
depth beckons.

I'm a frontiers person
once again;
the perpetual pioneer.

Lonely

Riverplace
they call it,
the new shopping mall,
resplendent, teeming,
all dressed up
for Christmas.

My feet are tired
but I don't go home.
I find a bench, a place
beside a solitary man.
I sense there's something,
I feel it, something
he has a need to tell.

Immediately, but shyly,
tentatively, he says:
"My wife died just
two months ago."

Anniversaries

Anniversaries are
thinking places, thanking places,
where one may reflect and review,
recollect and renew—taste and savor
all that's been, the better
to receive all that is to
be.

Anniversaries are
breathing spaces, healing places,
where one may pause and
set one's burden down,
not to abandon, but to
grasp it once again
with greater courage and resolve.

Anniversaries are
milestones, where one may be
repossessed by the goodness
of God.

Reverie

There are times
for doing nothing,
but be sure you do it well—

and listen.

For God,
in silent spaces,
has something great
to tell.

He Hanged Himself

He hanged himself
on a strap, they say.
He did it on the El.
But not in a moment,
nor even a day;
it took him many years.

He lost a dream,
grew old on routine,
then let his rut become his grave.

Don't fault the train.
If it hadn't happened there
he'd have found some other way,
for in the death of a dream
dies everything.

Retired

Retired.
It sounds like such a
damning word.
But today I've made my truce
with it; I am resolved
to remember what I've always affirmed—
that heaven is my Home.

My clock-timed work
has been but interim employment.
My full-time task remains the same,
to praise my God in righteousness,
peace and joy forever.

Retired? Returned!

Autobiography

If you should ask me,
"Who are you right now?
Where are you?
What road have you taken?
What have you become?"
I needn't give you fifty pages,
or even five, or one.
My check stubs are enough.

The Seed

We swim together,
my granddaughter and I
(she's eight),
so I telephoned
on this warm August day:
"Will you be ready when I come?"
And she was.

As I turned the corner
I spied her from a distance,
bright orange bathing suit,
curly dark head bent over a book,
intent on her reading.

The sound of the horn is usually sufficient
to bring her bounding toward me,
but not today.
Slowly, like one interrupted in a dream,
open book in hand, she came.

"Oh, Granddaddy," she exclaimed,
"I'm reading the most beautiful book!"
"What is it?" I asked.
The Wind in the Willows," she replied.
"That is beautiful," I said.
"I know quite a lot about it."

"I don't understand all the words,"
she continued, "but I like their sound,
like 'full-fed river.' "
"Oh, yes," I answered,
"and it means that hundreds
of brooks and creeks and smaller rivers
keep feeding the big river,
sending it toward the ocean."

"And what does i-n-s-a-t-i-a-b-l-e spell?"
"Insatiable," I said.
And she: "Listen to this,
'the insatiable sea,' isn't
that beautiful?"
And we talked about its meaning.

"And don't you like the sound of
The Wind in the Willows?" she continued.
"Don't you think it's a little like
'the last of the light of the sun
that had died in the west
still lived for one song more
in a thrush's breast'?"
(Lines from Robert Frost
which we'd struggled to memorize
a few days before.)

A seed had been sown, I knew,
the seed of appreciation and love
for the good, the beautiful,
and the true.

And I was glad.

Small Change

A wise friend decided
to live in community with others
rather than all alone.

"Oh, I can call a lawyer," she said;
"a doctor, a relative,
a policeman or a friend;
I know where there's help
in times of crisis.
But with whom can I be impulsive?

"Who will be there when I lift
back the curtain and say, 'Look,
a nuthatch on the tree trunk!
I wonder, will it rain today?
(I hate that announcer!)
Oh, see those northern lights!
My, but the days are getting short!
Our first snow of the season,
let's walk a little tonight!' "

For the daily commerce of living
—and especially at the
exclamation points!—we need the
small change of small talk.

Two Journeys

I was seventy,
setting out for Oregon,
with four thousand miles before me
and mountain passes to conquer,
and I was proud.

How many my age
dare this? I thought.

Then, just three blocks from home,
I saw him, my familiar friend,
tapping, tapping, tapping with his white cane
into another precarious day.

How dwarfed I felt by this, my teacher.
I watched him reach out for life's
challenge and seize it
in his hand.

All Must Fall

We sat on the bank
high above the crystal lake,
my beloved and I.

It was August
and one leaf fell,
just one,
but as it fell,
it spoke.

We thought we heard it say,
"All leaves must fall,
come September and October.
All must fall."

It is far past August
in our life together—
at least November.

Dear Lord of falling leaves,
of far-spent days and flowing rivers,
help us, your frail and fragile ones,
to look serenely into the sunset glory
of this, your given day.

My Country

My country, my dear homeland,
is sick when she's a bastion
for the rich and no refuge for the poor;
when fulfillment is a luxury for the few
and hope dies of starvation.

In heartless success
is failure.

Servant

"I am among you as one who serves."
Could He be back in the kitchen,
with the struggle and sweat and steam and din?

Would He shut himself out
of the glitter and glamour,
away from the partaking of sumptious dishes,
among bus boys and waiters,
dishwashers and cooks?

Would He be with all these,
without whom there'd be no banquet set?
And all these years have I been tipping Him
and never known?

Help Us to Let Go

I forgot my glasses today,
left them at a friend's house;
went to get them and forgot my hat;
went to get the hat, and on the way
met an acquaintance of many years,
remembered the face, but forgot the name.
I looked for an excuse.
"I'm old!" I said, "old, old, old!"
And I was angry
and sad.
Then I remembered
some things I'd forgotten I knew:

Forgetfulness is a gift,
one of the best of our gift-giving God.
Without it, what would we do?
How could we travel this day's journey
crushed by the burden of the past,
broken under the unbearable load?

So, dear God, help us to let go;
make us ready to relinquish
the painful baggage of yesterday—
the slurs and slaps, the burns and bruises.
School us in purposeful forgetting.

Toughest Fact

Morning has broken,
long shadows are receding;
time for today's resolution:

With the Spirit's help
I will remember that the toughest,
most resilient and tenacious,
most stubborn and unyielding
fact that I'll encounter this day
is the eternal and all-embracing
love of God.

God's Perennials

The longer I live with unanswerables
the more I see them as God's perennials—
his invitation to walk by faith.

The more I know of God's love
the greater my tolerance of ambiguities
and the fewer certainties I need.

What I Don't Like About Jesus

Let me tell you
what I don't like
about Jesus.

He calls me to follow;
I like to run around.
He lets me see a single step,
and sometimes even less than that;
I like to know the end.

I choose to travel
by sunlight or headlight;
He gives me only starlight.

I like to set the pace;
he asks me to hurry, or worse—
sometimes to wait.

He embarrasses me and gets me
into trouble; he sometimes
makes a scene.

And just when I feel strong
he calls me to a cross;
I want a crown.

The Music of the Mind

We spoke of heritage,
of things worth passing on.
The talk turned toward
selective memorization:
how wise it is to stock
the cupboards of the mind
with things that feed the heart.

The Reason

The reason old people
sometimes talk too much
is that everything
reminds them of something.
It's as simple as this:
They've lived.

For His Age

In my journey
from child back to child
I trip over thresholds.
Most troublesome is the one
called "for his age."

My doctor writes
of my general health:
"Excellent for his age."
It seems that whatever
is said to describe me,
three more words are required.
They qualify everything.

But I smile
as I remember:
They used to say the same
many long years ago:
"My, but he's beginning
to eat well with a spoon
for his age."

Time—
once I'd had too little;
now I've had too much.
Once I was a needy person;
now I am again.
Or have I always been?

Lord, I Saw Two

I watched them today
on the merry-go-round,
waited for their smiles,
their waving hands,
each time around.

To others, one child
and one adult;
to me, two children.
No longer my grandchild and her mother,
my daughter
and her daughter—
but two children,
riding the merry-go-round,
laughing.

One child,
but I saw two:
memory's trick photography
deepening joy and sorrow,
leaving me more exposed—
the price and pleasure
of the passing years.

Lord, I saw two:
for choicest wine left to the last
I thank you.

Saturday Morning

Lord, you know,
I've been straightening my desk,
and I needn't tell you
I'm a piler, not a filer,
and if I were a filer
I'd still lose things—
alphabetically, I mean.

So, Lord, as you once brooded
over primeval chaos
let your Spirit brood today
over this clutter
which is my life,
lest I lose myself
and you,
the Eternal Best.

Riches

"That's a pretty necktie you're wearing."
She paused, then added wistfully,
"That's one of the things I miss—
buying neckties for Elmer."

The years are good to her:
at eighty-three, grace and beauty
still are hers. And yet
she lives with sadness as she walks
the path of memory.

She can't help Elmer,
but me—she helps me see the treasures
on my street, riches
in humble wrappings.

The Hardest Part

The longer I live
the more assured I am
that God leaves the hardest part
till last—to stay alive
until I die.

I'm tempted to withdraw
a little every day,
to retreat into myself,
until I'm caught in the slowly
swirling current of
less and less.

I need God's constant help
to "fight the good fight"
and stay involved another day.

Memory

As I grow old
I'm more and more surprised
at how much I see
with my eyes closed.

I never knew
how rich and diverse
my picture-bank would be,
how many meanings have become
a part of me.

Is it more and more past
meeting less and less future,
or is it a deeper present?

Soon, perhaps, I'll know.
Meanwhile high drama plays
behind my aging eyelids
and I'm almost never bored.

And a Half

She's two and a half.
I like that "and a half"
because it's still important
enough to get a mention.

As for me
I daren't say
"seventy-seven and a half"—
they'd think me strange.
They'd say
if they're good at fractions:
"There he goes again,
mentioning that
one hundred fifty-fourth
of his life span.

For her
the "and a half"
is just one-fifth of all her days.
We elders are full of days.
This is the changed perspective
of the rushing years.

God Knows

"Time to come in now!"—
the mellow voice of love in the
darkening dusk of a distant day,
my barefoot, carefree days
of firefly lanterns,
cricket-chirped curfews
and the serious business of play.

No harshness to remember,
but firmness born of care,
the loving care of Mother;
she knew how much we liked to play.

"Time to come in now!"
I seem to hear God say
in the deepening dusk of my
sunset day.

God knows how much I want to stay.

Lost

"And how do the sheep get lost?"
the city dweller asked.
"Oh," said the friendly shepherd,
"they just put their heads down
and nibble themselves lost."

My Lord, it's now past noon,
and I've nibbled my way
from trivia to trivia
and don't know where I am.
Have mercy, redeem this heads-down day,
and put me on the trail again.

As I Bow

When I was young
I lived beneath a dappled sky.
A question here, a problem there,
but mostly sky. Life seemed
human-sized
and this a manageable world.

Today, with questions dwarfing
answers everywhere,
from east to west and north
to south,
I bow before the mystery, and
as I bow
I bend.

Nebo

"And Moses went up . . . to Mount Nebo. . . .
And the LORD showed him all the land,
. . . And the LORD said to him, . . . I have let you see it
. . . but you shall not go over there."
Deuteronomy 34:1-4

Moses went up
but he couldn't go in
because long ago
he shrank back.

The Lord shows me my Nebo,
my mountain of unlived life,
all that I feared to be.
He lets me know the story I wouldn't tell,
the song I didn't sing, the gift I didn't bring,
the hand I feared to take, the word I spurned
to speak when I shrank back
in self-protecting unbelief
or dull indifference.

He shows me why
my world is smaller now
than it was meant to be.

Celebration

Husband and wife
for more than a half-century,
but more than that—friends
from first to last, enjoying
one another.

But now they're frail.

We met them this morning;
they called to us:
Three good days and three good nights
we've had, and so
we're celebrating!

When joy is in the heart,
it will have its way;
if it can't have the loaf,
it celebrates the crumb.

Years Are Kettles

I like soup,
especially the second day:
Simmering is important.

Only simmered knowledge
has enough of living flavor
to qualify as wisdom.

Years are kettles.
They hold the goodness
of recollected joy and sadness.

People say I'm old.
That's all right with me
as long as simmering contentment
leaves its mellow residue.

Two Words

Two words I'd leave
to those who are coming after:
Expect more!

Expect to see more light
in what you've understood;
more beauty in all
you still admire;
more truth in all
you've long believed;
more goodness in all
you've learned to love.

Three with a Secret

"Lazarus, come forth!"
our Lord had said, and he came
to live on earth again.

I think of Lazarus, and wonder,
what was it like for him
to have glimpsed the other side?
Did he become a misfit then?
Did they make fun of him?

And was he absent-minded?
Was he known to chuckle when those beside him
were over-solemn about trite and trivial things?
Was he out of step like that?

Did he hear of the gossip from Nain,
of the widow's son and the funeral that never happened?
And what of the young daughter in the household
of Jairus? Did he hear her story too?

Most of all, I wonder, did they find each other
and beat a path to a familiar place
because they liked to be together,
these three, with their incommunicable
secret?

Home Sounds

I'm getting old;
eleven twenty, my life clock says.
It's getting late,
and later,
and I hear Home sounds.

Thank you, God,
in this late hour
that you are here
and there.